Environment and Art in Catholic Worship

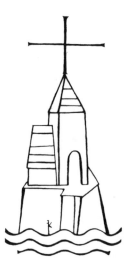

November 1977

Bishops' Committee on the Liturgy
National Conference of Catholic Bishops

Cover art: Frank Kacmarcik

The photographs were selected by the editorial
committee assembled for this publication by the
Bishops' Committee on the Liturgy.

ISBN 1-55586-563-1

FOREWORD

The following statement on art and environment in Catholic worship has been designated as a companion to the 1972 statement of the Bishops' Committee on the Liturgy entitled "Music in Catholic Worship." It is the result of a cooperative effort on the part of the Federation of Diocesan Liturgical Commissions and the Bishops' Committee to provide principles for those involved in preparing liturgical space for the worship of the Christian assembly.

The publication of the General Instruction of the Roman Missal and subsequent liturgical rites and documents along with the pastoral experience of implementing post-Vatican II reforms place us in a position to reexamine existing places of worship and to make informed decisions about their appropriateness. Furthermore, an awareness of liturgical needs and objectives, now clearer than a decade ago, provide guiding principles for the preparation of new places of worship.

This statement of the Bishops' Committee on the Liturgy will be of use not only to bishops and their diocesan liturgical commissions, architects and their liturgical consultants, but to all involved in the Church's worship. Everyone called to worship must be concerned about the vital role art and environment play in that central action of the community of faith, the household of the Lord.

Archbishop John Quinn
Chairman
Bishops' Committee on the Liturgy

November 2, 1977

ENVIRONMENT
AND ART IN CATHOLIC WORSHIP

1. Faith involves a good tension between
human modes of expressive communications
and God himself, whom our human tools can
never adequately grasp. God transcends. God
is mystery. God cannot be contained in or
confined by any of our words or images or
categories.

2. While our words and art forms cannot
contain or confine God, they can, like the
world itself, be icons, avenues of approach,
numinous presences, ways of touching without
totally grasping or seizing. Flood, fire, the rock,
the sea, the mountain, the cloud, the political
situations and institutions of succeeding
periods — in all of them Israel touched the face
of God, found help for discerning a way,
moved toward the reign of justice and peace.
Biblical faith assures us that God covenants a
people through human events and calls the
covenanted people to shape human events.

3. And then in Jesus, the Word of God is
flesh: "This is what we proclaim to you: what
was from the beginning, what we have heard,
what we have seen with our eyes, what we
have looked upon and our hands have touched
— we speak of the word of life."[1]

4. Christians have not hesitated to use every human art in their celebration of the saving work of God in Jesus Christ, although in every historical period they have been influenced, at times inhibited, by cultural circumstances. In the resurrection of the Lord, all things are made new. Wholeness and healthiness are restored, because the reign of sin and death is conquered. Human limits are still real and we must be conscious of them. But we must also praise God and give God thanks with the human means we have available. God does not need liturgy; people do, and people have only their own arts and styles of expression with which to celebrate.

5. Like the covenant itself, the liturgical celebrations of the faith community (Church) involve the whole person. They are not purely religious or merely rational and intellectual exercises, but also human experiences calling on all human faculties: body, mind, senses, imagination, emotions, memory. Attention to these is one of the urgent needs of contemporary liturgical renewal.

6. Historically, music has enjoyed a preeminence among the arts of public worship, and there is no clear evidence to justify denying it the same place today. The Bishops' Committee on the Liturgy, therefore, published guidelines (*Music in Catholic Worship*, 1972) encouraging attention to music, both instrumental and

choral/vocal. This companion booklet, *Environment and Art in Catholic Worship,* offers guidelines to encourage the other arts necessary for a full experience in public worship. The two booklets, therefore, should be used together, complementing one another, by those responsible for planning and conducting liturgical celebrations. For that reason, music is excluded from the specific concerns of the following pages.

7. If we maintain that no human words or art forms can contain or exhaust the mystery of God's love, but that all words and art forms can be used to praise God in the liturgical assembly, then we look for criteria to judge music, architecture, and the other arts in relation to public worship.[2]

8. The reason for offering principles to guide rather than blueprints to follow was stated clearly by the Council fathers: "The Church has not adopted any particular style of art as her very own; it has admitted styles from every period according to the natural talents and circumstances of peoples, and the needs of the various rites. Thus, in the course of the centuries, she has brought into being a treasury of art which must be carefully preserved. The art of our own days, coming from every race and region, shall also be given free scope in the Church, provided that it adorns the sacred buildings and holy rites with due reverence

and honor; thereby it is enabled to contribute its own voice to that wonderful chorus of praise. . . ."[3]

I. THE WORSHIP OF GOD AND ITS REQUIREMENTS

LITURGY AND TRADITION

9. Liturgy has a special and unique place in the life of Christians in the local churches, their communities of faith. Each Church gathers regularly to praise and thank God, to remember and make present God's great deeds, to offer common prayer, to realize and celebrate the kingdom of peace and justice. That action of the Christian assembly is liturgy.

10. Common traditions carried on, developed and realized in each community make liturgy an experience of the Church which is both local and universal. The roots as well as the structure of its liturgical celebrations are biblical and ecclesial, asserting a communion with believers of all times and places. This tradition furnishes the symbol language of that action, along with structures and patterns refined through the centuries of experience, and gives the old meanings new life in our time, our place, with our new knowledge, talents, competencies, arts. Therefore, this celebration

is that of a community at a given place and time, celebrated with the best of its resources, talents and arts in the light of our own tradition.[4]

A CLIMATE OF HOSPITALITY

11. As common prayer and ecclesial experience, liturgy flourishes in a climate of hospitality: a situation in which people are comfortable with one another, either knowing or being introduced to one another; a space in which people are seated together, with mobility, in view of one another as well as the focal points of the rite, involved as participants and *not* as spectators.[5]

THE EXPERIENCE OF MYSTERY

12. The experience of mystery which liturgy offers is found in its God-consciousness and God-centeredness. This involves a certain beneficial tension with the demands of hospitality, requiring a manner and an environment which invite contemplation (seeing beyond the face of the person or the thing, a sense of the holy, the numinous, mystery). A simple and attractive beauty in everything that is used or done in liturgy is the most effective invitation to this kind of experience. One should be able to sense something special (and nothing trivial) in everything that is seen and heard, touched and smelled, and tasted in liturgy.

13. Incarnation, the paschal mystery and the Holy Spirit in us are faith's access to the transcendence, holiness, otherness of God. An action like liturgy, therefore, has special significance as a means of relating to God, or responding to God's relating to us. This does not mean that we have "captured" God in our symbols. It means only that God has graciously loved us on our own terms, in ways corresponding to our condition. Our response must be one of depth and totality, of authenticity, genuineness, and care with respect to everything we use and do in liturgical celebration.

THE OPENING UP OF SYMBOLS

14. Every word, gesture, movement, object, appointment must be real in the sense that it is our own. It must come from the deepest understanding of ourselves (not careless, phony, counterfeit, pretentious, exaggerated, etc.). Liturgy has suffered historically from a kind of minimalism and an overriding concern for efficiency, partly because sacramental causality and efficacy have been emphasized at the expense of sacramental signification. As our symbols tended in practice to shrivel up and petrify, they became much more manageable and efficient. They still "caused," were still "efficacious" even though they had often ceased to signify in the richest, fullest sense.

15. Renewal requires the opening up of our symbols, especially the fundamental ones of bread and wine, water, oil, the laying on of hands, until we can experience all of them as authentic and appreciate their symbolic value.

THE PERSON-COMMUNAL EXPERIENCE

16. A culture which is oriented to efficiency and production has made us insensitive to the symbolic function of persons and things. Also, the same cultural emphasis on individuality and competition has made it more difficult for us to appreciate the liturgy as a *personal-communal* experience. As a consequence, we tend to identify anything private and individual as "personal." But, by inference, anything communal and social is considered impersonal. For the sake of good liturgy, this misconception must be changed.

17. To identify liturgy as an important *personal-communal* religious experience is to see the virtue of simplicity and commonness in liturgical texts, gestures, music, etc.
This is easier said than done. But it does require a persevering effort to respect the Church's mind in terms of its common feelings and simplicity, for example, by not drowning the action in a flood of words or by not making the action more complex than necessary in order to signify the gospel essentials.

18. An important part of contemporary Church renewal is the awareness of the community's recognition of the sacred. Environment and art are to foster this awareness. Because different cultural and subcultural groups in our society may have quite different styles of artistic expression, one cannot demand any universal sacred forms.[6]

QUALITY AND APPROPRIATENESS

19. This is not to say that liturgy makes no demand upon architecture, music and the other arts. To be true to itself and to protect its own integrity, liturgy must make demands. Basically, its demands are two: *quality* and *appropriateness*. Whatever the style or type, no art has a right to a place in liturgical celebration if it is not of high quality and if it is not appropriate.[7]

20. *Quality* is perceived only by contemplation, by standing back from things and really trying to *see* them, trying to let them speak to the beholder. Cultural habit has conditioned the contemporary person to look at things in a more pragmatic way: "What is it worth?" "What will it do?" Contemplation sees the hand stamp of the artist, the honesty and care that went into an object's making, the pleasing form and color and texture. Quality means love and care in the making of something, honesty and genuineness with any

materials used, and the artist's special gift in producing a harmonious whole, a well-crafted work. This applies to music, architecture, sculpture, painting, pottery making, furniture making, as well as to dance, mime or drama — in other words, to any art form that might be employed in the liturgical environment or action.

21. *Appropriateness* is another demand that liturgy rightfully makes upon any art that would serve its action. The work of art must be appropriate in two ways: 1) it must be capable of bearing the weight of mystery, awe, reverence, and wonder which the liturgical action expresses; 2) it must clearly *serve* (and not interrupt) ritual action which has its own structure, rhythm and movement.

22. The first point rules out anything trivial and self-centered, anything fake, cheap or shoddy, anything pretentious or superficial. That kind of appropriateness, obviously, is related to quality. But it demands more than quality. It demands a kind of transparency, so that we see and experience both the work of art and something beyond it.

23. The second point (to serve) refers both to the physical environment of public worship and to any art forms which might be employed as part of the liturgical action (e.g., ritual movement, gestures, audio-visuals, etc.).

THE SERVING ENVIRONMENT

24. By environment we mean the larger space in which the action of the assembly takes place. At its broadest, it is the setting of the building in its neighborhood, including outdoor spaces. More specifically it means the character of a particular space and how it affects the action of the assembly. There are elements in the environment, therefore, which contribute to the overall experience, e.g., the seating arrangement, the placement of liturgical centers of action, temporary decoration, light, acoustics, spaciousness, etc. The environment is appropriate when it is beautiful, when it is hospitable, when it clearly invites and needs an assembly of people to complete it. Furthermore, it is appropriate when it brings people close together so that they can see and hear the entire liturgical action, when it helps people feel involved and become involved. Such an environment works with the liturgy, not against it.

THE SERVICE OF THE ARTS

25. If an art form is used in liturgy it must aid and serve the action of liturgy since liturgy has its own structure, rhythm and pace: a gathering, a building up, a climax, and a descent to dismissal. It alternates between persons and groups of persons, between sound and silence, speech and song, movement and stillness, proclamation and reflection, word and action. The art form must never seem to

interrupt, replace, or bring the course of liturgy to a halt. If one uses film, for example, in such a way that one seems to be saying, "We will stop the liturgy for a few moments now in order to experience this art form," then that use is inappropriate. If, however, an art form is used to enhance, support and illumine a part or parts of the liturgical action or the whole action, it can be both appropriate and rewarding.

26. A major and continuing educational effort is required among believers in order to restore respect for competence and expertise in all the arts and a desire for their best use in public worship. This means winning back to the service of the Church professional people whose places have long since been taken by "commercial" producers, or volunteers who do not have the appropriate qualifications. Both sensitivity to the arts and willingness to budget resources for these are the conditions of progress so that quality and appropriateness can be real.

II. THE SUBJECT OF LITURGICAL ACTION: THE CHURCH

27. To speak of environmental and artistic requirements in Catholic worship, we have to begin with ourselves — we who are the Church, the baptized, the initiated.

THE ASSEMBLY OF BELIEVERS
28. Among the symbols with which liturgy deals, none is more important than this assembly of believers. It is common to use the same name to speak of the building in which those persons worship, but that use is misleading. In the words of ancient Christians, the building used for worship is called *domus ecclesiae*, the house of the Church.

THE ACTION OF THE ASSEMBLY
29. The most powerful experience of the sacred is found in the celebration and the persons celebrating, that is, it is found in the action of the assembly: the living words, the living gestures, the living sacrifice, the living meal. This was at the heart of the earliest liturgies. Evidence of this is found in their architectural floor plans which were designed as general gathering spaces, spaces which allowed the whole assembly to be part of the action.

30. Because liturgical celebration is the

worship action of the entire Church, it is desirable that persons representing the diversity of ages, sexes, ethnic and cultural groups in the congregation should be involved in planning and ministering in the liturgies of the community. Special competencies in music, public reading, and any other skills and arts related to public worship should be sought, respected and used in celebration. Not only the planners and ministers, however, are active in the liturgy. The entire congregation is an active component. There is no audience, no passive element in the liturgical celebration. This fact alone distinguishes it from most other public assemblies.

31. The assembly's celebration, that is, celebration in the midst of the faith community, by the whole community, is the normal and normative way of celebrating any sacrament or other liturgy. Even when the communal dimension is not apparent, as sometimes in communion for the sick or for prisoners, the clergy or minister function within the context of the entire community.

32. The action of the assembly is also unique since it is not merely a "celebration of life," reflecting all of the distinctions stemming from color, sex, class, etc. Quite the contrary, liturgy requires the faith community to set aside all those distinctions and divisions and

classifications. By doing this the liturgy celebrates the reign of God, and as such maintains the tension between what is (the status quo of our daily lives) and what must be (God's will for human salvation — liberation and solidarity). This uniqueness gives liturgy its key and central place in Christian life as seen from the perspective of an actual community. Just as liturgy makes its own demands on the environment and the arts, so too, does the assembly. When the assembly gathers with its own varied background, there is a commonness demanded which stems from our human condition. The commonality here seeks the best which people can bring together rather than what is compromised or less noble. For the assembly seeks its own expression in an atmosphere which is beautiful, amidst actions which probe the entire human experience. This is what is most basic and most noble. It is what the assembly seeks in order to express the heart of the Church's liturgy.

CONTEMPORARY

33. Contemporary art forms belong to the liturgical expressions of the assembly as surely as the art forms of the past. The latter are part of our common memory, our communion (which extends over time as well as over geographical boundaries). Contemporary art is our own, the work of artists of our time and place, and belongs in our

16

celebrations as surely as we do. If liturgy were to incorporate only the acceptable art of the past, conversion, commitment and tradition would have ceased to live. The assembly should, therefore, be equally unhesitating in searching out, patronizing and using the arts and media of past and present. Because it is symbolic communication, liturgy is more dependent on past tradition than many human activities are. Because it is the action of a contemporary assembly, it has to clothe its basically traditional structures with the living flesh and blood of our times and our arts.

BEAUTIFUL

34. Because the assembly gathers in the presence of God to celebrate his saving deeds, liturgy's climate is one of awe, mystery, wonder, reverence, thanksgiving and praise. So it cannot be satisfied with anything less than the *beautiful* in its environment and in all its artifacts, movements, and appeals to the senses.[8] Admittedly difficult to define, the beautiful is related to the sense of the numinous, the holy. Where there is evidently no care for this, there is an environment basically unfriendly to mystery and awe, an environment too casual, if not careless, for the liturgical action. In a world dominated by science and technology, liturgy's quest for the beautiful is a particularly necessary contribution to full and balanced human life.

35. To gather intentionally in God's presence is to gather our total selves, our complete persons — a "living sacrifice." Other human activities tend to be more incomplete, specialized, and to claim one or the other facet of ourselves, lives, talents, roles. Liturgy is total, and therefore must be much more than a merely rational or intellectual exercise. Valid tradition reflects this attention to the whole person. In view of our culture's emphasis on reason, it is critically important for the Church to reemphasize a more total approach to the human person by opening up and developing the non-rational elements of liturgical celebration: the concerns for feelings of conversion, support, joy, repentance, trust, love, memory, movement, gesture, wonder.

SINFUL

36. The Church is a church of sinners, and the fact that God forgives, accepts and loves sinners places the liturgical assembly under a fundamental obligation to be honest and unpretentious, without deceit or affectation, in all it does. If all distinctions have been stripped away, then basic honesty has to be carried through in all the words, gestures and movements, art forms, objects, furnishings of public worship. Nothing which pretends to be other than it is has a place in celebration, whether it is a person, cup, table or sculpture.

37. Different ministries in such an assembly do not imply "superiority" or "inferiority." Different functions are necessary in the liturgy as they are in any human, social activity. The recognition of different gifts and talents and the ordination, institution or delegation for the different services required (priest, reader, acolyte, musician, usher, etc.) is to facilitate worship. These are services to the assembly and those who perform them are servants of God who render services to the assembly. Those who perform such ministries are indeed servants of the assembly.

38. The liturgical assembly, as presented, is Church, and as Church is servant to the world. It has a commitment to be sign, witness, and instrument of the reign of God. That commitment must be reflected and implemented not only in the individual lives of its members but also in the community's choices and in its use of its money, property and other resources. Liturgical buildings and spaces should have the same witness value. Their planning should involve representatives of oppressed and disadvantaged parts of the communities in which they are located.

III. A HOUSE FOR THE CHURCH'S LITURGICAL CELEBRATIONS

39. The congregation, its liturgical action, the furniture and the other objects it needs for its liturgical action — these indicate the necessity of a space, a place, a hall, or a building for the liturgy. It will be a place for praying and singing, for listening and speaking — a place for human interaction and active participation — where the mysteries of God are recalled and celebrated in human history. The servant nature of the Church in relation to the rest of the community in its area (and in the world) invites it to consider the broader needs of the community, especially in the community's deprived, handicapped and suffering members, and therefore to consider a breadth of possible uses of its buildings.

PRIMARY DEMAND: THE ASSEMBLY
40. In no case, however, should this mean a lack of attention to the requirements of liturgical celebration or a yielding of the primary demands that liturgy must make upon the space: the gathering of the faith community in a participatory and hospitable atmosphere for word and eucharist, for initiation and reconciliation, for prayer and praise and song.

41. Such a space acquires a sacredness from the sacred action of the faith community which uses it. As a place, then, it becomes quite

naturally a reference and orientation point for believers. The historical problem of the church as a *place* attaining a dominance over the faith community need not be repeated as long as Christians respect the primacy of the living assembly.

42. The norm for designing liturgical space is the assembly and its liturgies. The building or cover enclosing the architectural space is a shelter or "skin" for a liturgical action. It does not have to "look like" anything else, past or present. Its integrity, simplicity and beauty, its physical location and landscaping should take into account the neighborhood, city and area in which it is built.

43. Many local Churches must use spaces designed and built in a former period, spaces which may now be unsuitable for the liturgy. In the renovation of these spaces for contemporary liturgical use, there is no substitute for an ecclesiology that is both ancient and modern in the fullest sense. Nor is there any substitute for a thorough understanding of ritual needs in human life and the varied liturgical tradition of the Church. With these competencies, a renovation can respect both the best qualities of the original structure and the requirements of contemporary worship.

44. Whether designing a new space for the liturgical action or renovating an old one, teamwork and preparation by the congregation (particularly its liturgy committee), clergy, architect and consultant (liturgy and art) are essential.[9] A competent architect should have the assistance of a consultant in liturgy and art both in the discussion stages of the project (dialogue with congregation and clergy as well as among themselves) and throughout the stages of design and building. Recent competitions in the design of buildings for liturgy have indicated the advantages of such consultation.

45. The congregation, or local Church, commonly acting through its delegates, is a basic and primary component in the team. The congregation's work is to acquaint the architect and consultant with its own self-image as Church and its sense of the larger community in which it exists. It is important for the congregation and clergy to recognize the area of their own competence. This will also define the limits beyond which they should not go. Respect for the competence of others in their respective fields is essential for good teamwork.

46. If a community has selected competent and skilled persons, they will receive from the architect and the consultant, a design which

will stimulate and inspire, as well as serve the assembly's needs as they have been described. When financial benefactors are involved, they have the same part in this process as the congregation and the clergy, subject to the same prior requirements of good liturgy.

47. A good architect will possess both the willingness to learn from the congregation and sufficient integrity not to allow the community's design taste or preference to limit the freedom necessary for a creative design. The architect will look to the congregation and clergy for an understanding of the character and purpose of the liturgical assembly. With that rapport, it is the architect's task to design the space, using contemporary materials and modes of construction, in dialogue with consultants who are expert in the areas of liturgical art, rites, acoustics and other specialized issues.

48. The liturgical-artistic consultant is an invaluable partner of the architect, for the purposes of space can be imagined and the place creatively designed only by a competent designer (architect) who is nourished with liturgy's tradition, its current shape, together with the appropriate furniture and other objects used. The feeling of liturgical action is as crucial as the craft of the designer in producing a worthy space and place.

49. One of the primary requirements of the
space is visibility of all in the assembly:
others in the congregation as well as
the principal focal point of the ritual action.

50. Visibility speaks more to the quality of
view than merely the mechanics of seeing. A
space must create a sense that what is seen is
proximate, important and personal. The
arrangement of the space should consider
levels of priority in what is seen, allowing
visual flow from one center of liturgical action
to another. Furthermore, the sense and variety
of light, artificial or natural, contribute greatly
to what is seen.

51. Audibility of all (congregation and
ministers) is another primary
requirement. A space that does not require
voice amplification is ideal. Where an
amplifying system is necessary, provision for
multiple microphone jacks should be made
(e.g., at the altar, ambo, chair, font, space
immediately in front of the congregation, and a
few spots through the congregation). Since the
liturgical space must accommodate both speech
and song, there must be a serious acoustical
consideration of the conflicting demands of
the two. The services of an acoustical engineer
can enable architect and builder to be aware of
certain disadvantages in rooms that are
exclusively "dry" or "live." A room designed

to deaden all sounds is doomed to kill liturgical participation.

THE SCALE OF A SPACE

52. The liturgical space should have a "good feeling" in terms of human scale, hospitality and graciousness. It does not seek to impress, or even less, to dominate, but its clear aim is to facilitate the public worship and common prayer of the faith community.

UNITY OF SPACE

53. Special attention must be given to the unity of the entire liturgical space. Before considering the distinction of roles within the liturgy, the space should communicate an integrity (a sense of oneness, of wholeness) and a sense of being the gathering place of the initiated community. Within that one space there are different areas corresponding to different roles and functions, but the wholeness of the total space should be strikingly evident.

54. Planning for a convergence of pathways to the liturgical space in a concourse or foyer or other place adequate for gathering before or after liturgies is recommended. In some climates this might be outdoors. Such a gathering-space can encourage introductions, conversations, the sharing of refreshments after a liturgy, the building of the kind of community sense and feeling recognized now to be a prerequisite of good celebration.

IV. THE ARTS AND THE BODY LANGUAGE OF LITURGY

55. Liturgical celebration, because of its public and corporate nature, and because it is an expression of the total person within a community, involves not only the use of a common language and ritual tradition, but also the use of a common place, common furnishings, common art forms and symbols, common gestures, movements and postures. But when one examines the quality of these common elements, one finds that an uncommon sensitivity is demanded. For these common elements create a tremendous impact on the assembly visually, environmentally and bodily. This section and those following will offer a basic orientation and some principles with regard to each of these elements. We will begin with the sense of the person in the space: the bodily movement.

PERSONAL GESTURES

56. The liturgy of the Church has been rich in a tradition of ritual movement and gestures. These actions, subtly, yet really, contribute to an environment which can foster prayer or which can distract from prayer. When the gestures are done in common, they contribute to the unity of the worshiping assembly. Gestures which are broad and full in both a visual and tactile sense, support the entire symbolic ritual. When the gestures are done by

the presiding minister, they can either engage the entire assembly and bring them into an even greater unity, or if done poorly, they can isolate.[10]

POSTURE

57. In an atmosphere of hospitality, posture will never be a marshalled, forced uniformity. It is important that the liturgical space can accommodate certain common postures: sitting for preparations, for listening, for silent reflection; standing for the gospel, solemn prayer, praise and acclamation; kneeling for adoration, penitential rites. Those who suffer from handicaps of one sort or another, must be carefully planned for so that they can participate in the liturgy without unnecessary strain or burden.

58. Attentiveness, expressed in posture and eye contact, is a requirement for full participation and involvement in the liturgy. It is part of one's share in the life of the community and something one owes the rest of the assembly. Because of this, a space and its seating should be so designed that one can see the places of the ritual action, but further, that these spaces cannot be so distant that eye contact is impossible, for eye contact is important in any act of ministry — in reading, in preaching, in leading the congregation in music and prayer. Not only are the ministers to be visible to all present, but among themselves

the faithful should be able to have visual contact, being attentive to one another as they celebrate the liturgy.

PROCESSIONS

59. Beyond seeing what is done, because good liturgy is a ritual action, it is important that worship spaces allow for movement.[11] Processions and interpretations through bodily movement (dance) can become meaningful parts of the liturgical celebration if done by truly competent persons in the manner that befits the total liturgical action. A procession should move from one place to another with some purpose (not simply around the same space), and should normally include the congregation, sometimes with stops or stations for particular prayers, readings, or actions. The design of the space and arrangement of the seating should allow for this sort of movement. There should be concern for the quality, the gracefulness, and the surety of this movement. Seating arrangements which prohibit the freedom of action to take place, are inappropriate.

60. In the general movement of the liturgical rite, the role of the one who presides is critical and central. The area of presiding should allow that person to be attentive to and present to the entire congregation, the other ministers, and each part of the liturgical action, even if not personally

leading the action at that moment.
The place should allow one to conduct the various ministers in their specific activity and roles of leadership, as well as the congregation in its common prayer.

61. In the above instances, audibility and visibility to all in the assembly are minimal requirements. The chair, the lectern and the altar should be constructed so that all can see and hear the person of the reader or the one who presides.

EASE OF MOVEMENT
62. The proper use of furniture and other objects which have a symbolic function is important in ritual action. These objects are next in importance to the people themselves and their total environment. They are part of a total rite which everyone present should be able to experience as fully as possible. Thus, their placement and use should allow for ease of movement.

V. FURNISHINGS
FOR LITURGICAL CELEBRATION

63. Because the Sunday eucharistic assembly
is the most fundamental ecclesial symbol, the
requirements of that celebration will have the
strongest claim in the provision of furnishings
for liturgy. Consequently, any liturgical space
must take into consideration not only the
general requirements of the assembly but also
the need for a feeling of contact with altar,
ambo and celebrant's chair.

64. This primacy of the eucharistic assembly,
however, should not discourage a liturgical life
of greater richness and variety in the local
Church. In planning construction, renovation
or refurnishing of liturgical spaces, baptism
and the other sacraments, morning and
evening prayer, services of the word, prayer
meetings and other community events should
be kept in mind.

65. When multi-functional use of the space is
indicated by the needs either of the faith
community or of the surrounding city, town or
rural area which the faith community services,
a certain flexibility or movability should be
considered even for the essential furnishings.
Great care, however, should be taken in the
design and care of movable furnishings that
none of the dignity, noble and simple beauty
proper to such objects is sacrificed. There is no

reason why a movable altar or ambo need have a flimsy, cheap or disposable appearance.

66. Normally the furnishings used in a liturgical celebration of any kind should be placed before the celebration begins and remain stationary during the celebration. Ritual action is not enhanced by the moving of furniture during a rite. A careful arrangement of furnishings is an integral part of liturgical planning.

DIGNITY AND BEAUTY

67. Consultation with persons who are experts, at least one in liturgy and one in the arts, is not a luxury but a necessity for those responsible for furnishing the liturgical space. Each piece of furniture has its own requirements, but at least two criteria are applicable to all of them, in fact, to any object used in any way in liturgy: 1) None should be made in such a way that it is far removed from the print of the human hand and human craft. When mass-produced items are chosen, care must be taken that they are truly suitable. Dignity and beauty in materials used, in design and form, in color and texture — these are concerns of artists for their work, for the furniture they build, and are not, unfortunately, the evident concerns of many mass manufacturers and merchandisers. 2) All furnishings taken together should possess a unity and harmony with each other and with the architecture of the place.

68. Benches or chairs for seating the assembly should be so constructed and arranged that they maximize feelings of community and involvement.[12] The arrangement should facilitate a clear view not only of the one who presides and the multiple focal points of reading, preaching, praying, music and movement during the rite, but also of other members of the congregation. This means striving for a seating pattern and furniture that do not constrict people, but encourage them to move about when it is appropriate.

69. Benches or chairs for the seating of those engaged in the ministry of music, instrumental or choral, should be so constructed and arranged that they have the advantages described above for congregational seating and also that they are clearly part of the assembly.[13] Yet, the ministers of music should be able to sing and play facing the rest of the assembly in order to elicit the participation of the community without distracting from the central action of the liturgy. The same should be said of an individual cantor or song leader.

THE CHAIR

70. Chairs or benches for the presiding minister and other ministers, should be so constructed and arranged that they too are clearly part of the one assembly, yet conveniently situated for the exercise of their

respective offices. The importance of the personal symbol and function of the one who presides in liturgical celebration should not be underrated or underplayed, because it is essential for good celebration. The chair of that person should be clearly in a presiding position, although it should not suggest either domination or remoteness.[14]

THE ALTAR

71.   The altar, the holy table, should be the most noble, the most beautifully designed and constructed table the community can provide.[15] It is the common table of the assembly, a symbol of the Lord, at which the presiding minister stands and upon which are placed the bread and wine and their vessels and the book. It is holy and sacred to this assembly's action and sharing, so it is never used as a table of convenience or as a resting place for papers, notes, cruets, or anything else. It stands free, approachable from every side, capable of being encircled. It is desirable that candles, cross, any flowers or other decoration in the area should not be so close to the altar as to constitute impediments to anyone's approach or movement around the common table.

72.   The altar is designed and constructed for the action of a community and the functioning of a single priest — not for concelebrants. The holy table, therefore, should not be elongated, but square or slightly rectangular,

an attractive, impressive, dignified, noble table, constructed with solid and beautiful materials, in pure and simple proportions. Its symbolic function, of course, is rendered negligible when there are other altars in sight. The liturgical space has room for but one.

73. The location of the altar will be central in any eucharistic celebration, but this does not mean it must be spatially in the center or on a central axis. In fact, an off-center location may be a good solution in many cases. Focus and importance in any celebration move with the movement of the rite. Placement and elevation must take into account the necessity of visibility and audibility for all.

THE AMBO

74. The ambo or lectern is a standing desk for reading and preaching (although preaching can be done from the chair or elsewhere).[16] One main ambo should be reserved for these functions and therefore not used by commentators, song leaders, etc. Like the altar, it should be beautifully designed, constructed of fine materials, and proportioned carefully and simply for its function. The ambo represents the dignity and uniqueness of the Word of God and of reflection upon that Word.

75. A very simple lectern, in no way competing or conflicting with the main ambo, and placed for the necessary visibility and

audibility, can be used by a cantor, song
leader, commentator, and reader of the
announcements. It should be located for easy
communication with both musicians and
congregation.

BAPTISTRY
76. To speak of symbols and of sacramental
signification is to indicate that immersion is the
fuller and more appropriate symbolic action in
baptism.[17] New baptismal fonts, therefore,
should be constructed to allow for the
immersion of infants, at least, and to allow for
the pouring of water over the entire body of a
child or adult. Where fonts are not so
constructed, the use of a portable one is
recommended.

77. The place of the font, whether it is an area
near the main entrance of the liturgical space or
one in the midst of the congregation, should
facilitate full congregational participation,
regularly in the Easter Vigil.[18] If the
baptismal space is in a gathering place or entry
way, it can have living, moving water, and
include provision for warming the water for
immersion. When a portable font is used, it
should be placed for maximum visibility and
audibility, without crowding or obscuring the
altar, ambo and chair.

EUCHARISTIC CHAPEL
78. The *celebration* of the eucharist is the focus

of the normal Sunday assembly. As such, the major space of a church is designed for this *action*. Beyond the celebration of the eucharist, the Church has had a most ancient tradition of reserving the eucharistic bread. The purpose of this reservation is to bring communion to the sick and to be the object of private devotion. Most appropriately, this reservation should be designated in a space designed for individual devotion. A room or chapel specifically designed and separate from the major space is important so that no confusion can take place between the celebration of the eucharist and reservation.[19] Active and static aspects of the same reality cannot claim the same human attention at the same time. Having the eucharist reserved in a place apart does not mean it has been relegated to a secondary place of no importance. Rather, a space carefully designed and appointed can give proper attention to the reserved sacrament.

79. This space should offer easy access from the porch areas, garden or street as well as the main space. The devotional character of the space should create an atmosphere of warmth while acknowledging the mystery of the Lord. It should support private meditation without distractions. If iconography or statuary are present, they should not obscure the primary focus of reservation.

THE TABERNACLE

80. The tabernacle, as a receptacle for the reservation of the eucharist, should be solid and unbreakable, dignified and properly ornamented.[20] It may be placed in a wall niche, on a pillar, eucharistic tower. It should not be placed on an altar for the altar is a place for action not for reservation. There should be only one tabernacle in a church building. A lamp should burn continuously near it.

RECONCILIATION CHAPEL

81. A room or rooms for the reconciliation of individual penitents may be located near the baptismal area (when that is at the entrance) or in another convenient place.[21] Furnishings and decoration should be simple and austere, offering the penitent a choice between face-to-face encounter or the anonymity provided by a screen, with nothing superfluous in evidence beyond a simple cross, table and bible. The purpose of this room is primarily for the celebration of the reconciliation liturgy; it is not a lounge, counseling room, etc. The word "chapel" more appropriately describes this space.

SACRISTY

82. A sacristy or vesting space should be located to favor the procession of cross, candles, book and ministers through the midst of the congregation to the altar area.

MUSICAL INSTRUMENTS

83. Because choir, instrumentalists and organ often function as an ensemble, they need to be located together in such a way that the organist can see the other musicians and the liturgical action directly or by means of a simple mirror.[22] Organ consoles can be detached from the pipework and their connection supplied by flexible means. This allows for movable consoles, which may be an advantage, especially when the liturgical space serves other functions as well. However, self-contained organs, where console and pipework are united in a single element, are a possibility also, and can be designed so that the whole organ is movable. Organs designed for liturgical rather than concert purposes need not be very large; they should not be grandiose or visually dominating. But they should be superior musically, and as with all artifacts, the instrument and its casework should be authentic, beautiful and coherent with its environment. Proper space must also be planned for other musical instruments used in liturgical celebrations.

VI. OBJECTS USED IN LITURGICAL CELEBRATION

84. Like the furniture, all other objects used in liturgical celebrations should be designed or selected in consultation with experts in both liturgy and art. Each should be not only suitable for its purpose but also capable of making a visual or other sensory contribution to the beauty of the action. The two principles cited above are applicable to everything employed in liturgy.

DUPLICATED AND MINIMIZED

85. There is a cultural tendency to minimize symbols and symbolic gestures and to cover them with a heavy curtain of texts, words and commentary. As a result there are two other problems in our use of objects in worship.

86. One problem is the tendency to duplicate signs and objects, a practice which seems to have multiplied in proportion to the symbols' diminution. (The converse is also true: the multiplication of symbols causes their very diminution.) A symbol claims human attention and consciousness with a power that seems to be adversely affected by overdose. For example, the multiplication of crosses in a liturgical space or as ornamentation on objects may lessen rather than increase attention to that symbol.

87. A second common problem in the use of symbolic objects is a tendency to "make up" for weak primary symbols by secondary ones. It is not uncommon for example, to make extensive and expensive efforts to enrich and enliven a Sunday eucharistic celebration without paying any attention to the bread that is used or to the sharing of the cup. Bread and wine are primary eucharistic symbols, yet peripheral elements frequently get more attention. It is important to focus on central symbols and to allow them to be expressed with the full depth of their vision. This may mean solutions which are less efficient and pragmatic.

THE CROSS

88. A cross is a basic symbol in any Christian liturgical celebration. The advantage of a processional cross with a floor standard, in contrast to one that is permanently hung or affixed to a wall, is that it can be placed differently according to the celebration and the other environmental factors.[23] While it is permissible for the cross to rest on the altar, it is preferable that it be elsewhere, not only for non-eucharistic liturgies but also so that in eucharistic celebrations the altar is used only for bread and wine and book.

CANDLESTICKS AND CANDLES

89. The same can be said of candlesticks and candles. When they are floor-standing, they

can be arranged differently from time to time. The number can be varied according to the season and feast and the solemnity of the celebration. Like the cross, the candles should be visible without impeding the sight of the altar, ambo, chair and action.[24]

90. The Easter Candle and its standard call for very special dimensions and design. They occupy a central location in the assembly during the Easter season and a place at the baptismal font thereafter.[25]

BOOKS
91. Any book which is used by an officiating minister in a liturgical celebration should be of a large (public, noble) size, good paper, strong design, handsome typography and binding.[26] The Book of the Gospels or lectionary, of course, is central and should be handled and carried in a special way. The other liturgical books of the Church, which contain the rites of our public worship tradition, are also worthy of venerable treatment and are a significant part of the liturgical environment. Each should be visually attractive and impressive. The use of pamphlets and leaflets detracts from the visual integrity of the total liturgical action. This applies not only to books used by ministers at the altar, chair and font, but also to those used in any other public or semipublic rite.

92. When a liturgical book is employed at a place other than altar or ambo, the book should be held by an assistant or acolyte so that the hands and body of the one who reads are free.

VESTMENTS

93. The wearing of ritual vestment by those charged with leadership in a ritual action is an appropriate symbol of their service as well as a helpful aesthetic component of the rite.[27] That service is a function which demands attention from the assembly and which operates in the focal area of the assembly's liturgical action. The color and form of the vestments and their difference from everyday clothing invite an appropriate attention and are part of the ritual experience essential to the festive character of a liturgical celebration.[28]

94. The more these vestments fulfill their function by their color, design and enveloping form, the less they will need the signs, slogans and symbols which an unkind history has fastened on them. The tendency to place symbols upon symbols seems to accompany the symbolic deterioration and diminution already discussed.[29]

95. Vesture may also be used appropriately on an altar or ambo or other objects at times, especially for festive occasions, not as "frontals" or "facades," but as decorative

covering which respects the integrity and
totality of the particular object.[30] The fabrics
used in these instances should be chosen
because of the quality of design, texture and
color.

VESSELS

96. In a eucharistic celebration, the vessels for
the bread and wine deserve special attention
and care.[31] Just as in other types of celebration
those objects which are central in the rite are a
natural focus. When the eucharistic assembly is
large, it is desirable not to have the additional
plates and cups necessary for communion on
the altar. A solution is to use one large
breadplate and either one large chalice or a
large flagon until the breaking of the bread. At
the fraction, any other chalices or plates
needed are brought to the altar. While the
bread is broken on sufficient plates for sharing,
the ministers of the cups pour from the flagon
into the communion chalices. The number
and design of such vessels will depend on
the size of the community they serve. To
eat and drink is of the essence of the symbolic
fullness of this sacrament. Communion
under one kind is an example of the
minimizing of primary symbols.

97. Like the plates and chalices or flagons, all
other vessels and implements used in the
liturgical celebration should be of such
quality and design that they speak of

the importance of the ritual action. Pitchers, vessels for holy oils, bowls, cruets, sprinklers, censers, baskets for collection, etc. — all are presented to the assembly in one way or another and speak well or ill of the deed in which the assembly is engaged.

IMAGES

98. Images in painting or sculpture, as well as tapestries, cloth hangings, banners and other permanent or seasonal decorations should be introduced into the liturgical space upon consultation with an art consultant.[32] Like the furniture and other objects used in worship, they become part of the environment and are subject to its criteria of quality and appropriateness. In addition, their appropriateness must take into account the current renewed emphasis on the action of the assembly. If instead of serving and aiding that action, they threaten it or compete with it, then they are unsuitable.

99. In a period of Church and liturgical renewal, the attempt to recover a solid grasp of Church and faith and rites involves the rejection of certain embellishments which have in the course of history become hindrances. In many areas of religious practice, this means a simplifying and a refocusing on primary symbols. In building, this effort has resulted in more austere interiors, with fewer objects on the walls and in the corners.

DECORATIONS

100. Many new or renovated liturgical
spaces, therefore, invite temporary decoration
for particular celebrations, feasts and seasons.
Banners and hangings of various sorts are both
popular and appropriate, as long as the nature
of these art forms is respected. They are
creations of forms, colors, and textures, rather
than signboards to which words must be
attached. Their purpose is to appeal to the
senses and thereby create an atmosphere and a
mood, rather than to impress a slogan upon
the minds of observers or deliver a verbal
message.

101. Although the art and decoration of the
liturgical space will be that of the local culture,
identifying symbols of particular cultures,
groups, or nations are not appropriate as
permanent parts of the liturgical environment.
While such symbols might be used for a
particular occasion or holiday, they should not
regularly constitute a part of the environment
of common prayer.

102. Flowers, plants and trees — genuine, of
course — are particularly apt for the decoration
of liturgical space, since they are of nature,
always discreet in their message, never cheap
or tawdry or ill-made. Decoration should never
impede the approach to or the encircling of the
altar or any of the ritual movement and action,
but there are places in most liturgical spaces

where it is appropriate and where it can be enhancing. The whole space is to be considered the arena of decoration, not merely the sanctuary.

103. Suitable decoration need not and should not be confined to the altar area, since the unity of the celebration space and the active participation of the entire assembly are fundamental principles. The negative aspect of this attention to the whole space invites a thorough housecleaning in which superfluities, things that have no use or are no longer used, are removed. Both beauty and simplicity demand careful attention to each piece of furniture, each object, each decorative element, as well as to the whole ensemble, so that there is no clutter, no crowding. These various objects and elements must be able to breathe and function without being smothered by excess.

AUDIOVISUALS

104. It is too early to predict the effect of contemporary audiovisual media — films, video tape, records, tapes — on the public worship of Christians. It is safe to say that a new church building or renovation project should make provision for screens and/or walls which will make the projection of films, slides and filmstrips visible to the entire assembly, as well as an audio system capable of fine electronic reproduction of sound. [33]

105.   There seems to be a parallel between the new visual media and the traditional function of stained glass. Now that the easily printed word has lost its grip on popular communication, the neglect of audiovisual possibilities is a serious fault. Skill in using these media in ways which will not reduce the congregation to an audience or passive state can be gained only by experience.

106.   Such media, of course, should never be used to replace essential congregational action. At least two ways in which they may be used to enhance celebration and participation are already apparent: 1) visual media may be used to create an environment for the liturgical action, surrounding the rite with appropriate color and form; 2) visual and audio media may be used to assist in the communication of appropriate content, a use which requires great delicacy and a careful, balanced integration into the liturgy taken as a whole.

VII. CONCLUSION

107.   When the Christian community gathers
to celebrate its faith and vision, it gathers to
celebrate what is most personally theirs and
most nobly human and truly Church. The
actions of the assembly witness the great deeds
God has done; they confirm an age-old
covenant. With such vision and depth of the
assembly can the environment be anything less
than a vehicle to meet the Lord and to
encounter one another? The challenge of our
environment is the final challenge of Christ:
We must make ready until he returns in glory.

NOTES

1. 1 John 1
2. Among the official conciliar and post conciliar documents which specifically address these questions are: The Constitution on the Sacred Liturgy (=CSL), Chapters 6 and 7; Instruction of the Congregation of Rites for the Proper Implementation of the Constitution on the Sacred Liturgy, Chapter 6; and the General Instruction of the Roman Missal (=GI), Chapters 5 and 6.
3. CSL no. 123.
4. GI Introduction nos. 6–15.
5. GI nos. 4, 5.
6. CSL no. 123.
7. GI no. 254.
8. GI no. 253.
9. CSL no. 126; GI no. 258.
10. The Directory for Masses With Children (=DMC) bases the importance of the development of gestures, postures and actions in the liturgy on the fact that liturgy, by its nature, is the activity of the entire person (see no. 33).
11. See Holy Communion and Worship of the Eucharist Outside Mass (=EOM) nos. 101–108; DMC no. 34.
12. GI no. 273.
13. GI no. 274.
14. GI no. 271.
15. GI nos. 259–270; Appendix to GI no. 263.
16. GI no. 272.
17. Rite of Baptism for Children (=BC), Introduction no.
18. Ibid. no. 25.
19. GI no. 276.
20. GI no. 277.
21. Rite of Penance, nos. 12, 18b; Bishops' Committee on the Liturgy Newsletter 1965–1975, p. 450.
22. GI nos. 274, 275; Music in Catholic Worship no. 38.
23. GI nos. 84, 270; Appendix to GI no. 270.
24. GI no. 269, EOM no. 85.
25. BC no. 25.

26. Bishops' Committee on the Liturgy Newsletter 1965–1975, p. 417.
27. GI nos. 297–310; Appendix GI nos. 305–306.
28. GI nos. 308; Appendix GI no. 308.
29. GI no. 306.
30. GI no. 268.
31. GI nos. 289–296.
32. CSL no. 125; GI no. 278.
33. See DMC nos. 35–36.

ILLUSTRATIONS

In the following illustrations there is an attempt to give visual examples of principles found in the text.

While viewing the examples this fundamental truth should be kept in mind: When the Christian community gathers to celebrate its faith and vision, it gathers to celebrate what is most personally theirs and most nobly human and truly Church.

To identify liturgy as an
important personal
communal religious
experience is to see the
virtue of simplicity and
commonness.

4

Quality is perceived only by contemplation, by standing
back from things and really trying to see them, trying to let
them speak to the beholder.

5

Contemplation sees the hand stamp of the artist, the honesty
and care that went into an object's making, the pleasing form and
color and texture.

6

One should be able to sense something special in everything that is seen and heard, *touched* and smelled and tasted in liturgy.

The location of the altar will be central in any eucharistic celebration, but this does not mean it must be spacially in the center or on a central axis. (*9 before, 10 after renovation*)

11

Liturgy flourishes in a climate of hospitality: a situation in which people are comfortable with one another; a space in which people are seated in view of one another as well as the focal points of the rite.

In the renovation of spaces built in a former period there is no substitute for an ecclesiology that is both ancient and modern in the fullest sense. (*12 before, 13 after renovation*)

Contemporary art forms belong to the liturgical expressions of the assembly as surely as the art forms of the past. The latter are part of our common memory.

14

15

16

17

All furnishing taken together should possess a unity and harmony with each other and with the architecture of the place. (*16 before, 17 after with new eucharistic shrine, 19 expanded traditional confessional made into a chapel of reconciliation.*)

20

21

A renovation can respect both the best qualities of the original structure and the requirements of contemporary worship.

The altar is the common table of the assembly, a symbol of the Lord. It is designed and constructed for the action of a community and the functioning of a single priest. The holy table, therefore, should not be elongated, but square or slightly rectangular.

Most appropriately, the reservation of the Eucharist should be
designated in a space designed for individual devotion.

The chair of the priest should be clearly in a presiding position, although it should not suggest either domination or remoteness.

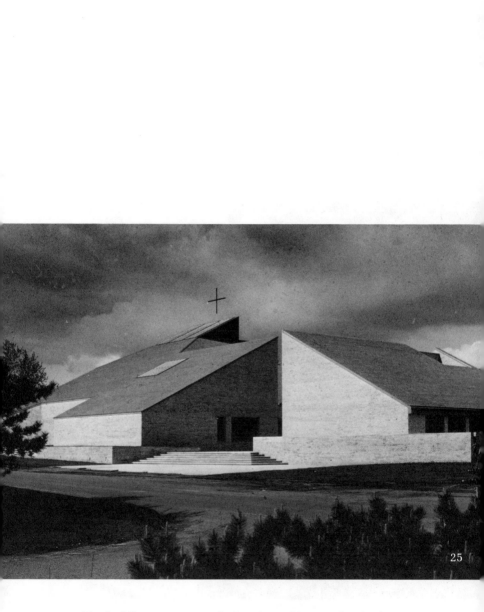

25

The building or cover enclosing the architectural space is a
shelter or "skin" for liturgical action. Its integrity,
simplicity and beauty, its physical location and
landscaping should take into account the neighborhood,
city and area in which it is built.

The place of the font, whether it is an area near the main entrance of the liturgical space or one in the midst of the congregation, should facilitate full congregational participation.

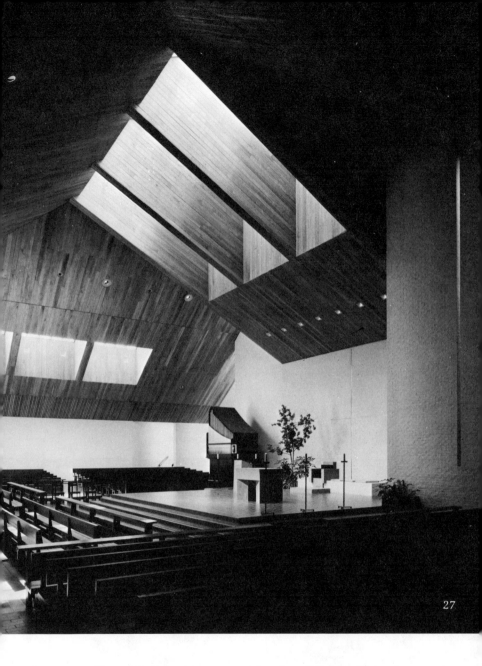

The environment is appropriate when it is beautiful, when
it is hospitable, when it clearly invites and needs an assembly
of people to complete it.

When candlesticks are floor-standing, they can be arranged
differently. The number can be varied according to the season
and feast and the solemnity of the celebration.
Flowers, plants and trees — genuine, of course — are
particularly apt for the decoration of liturgical space.

28

29

The tabernacle, as a receptacle
for the reservation of the
Eucharist, should be solid and
unbreakable, dignified and
properly ornamented. It may be
placed in a wall niche, on a
pillar, eucharistic tower.

30

The assembly cannot be satisfied with anything less than
the beautiful in its environment and in all its artifacts,
movements, and appeals to the senses.

This means the winning back to the service of the Church
professional people whose places have long since been
taken by "commercial" producers.

33

The advantage of a processional cross, in contrast to one that is permanently hung, is that it can be placed differently according to the celebration and the other environmental factors.

Contemporary art is our own, the work of artists of our time and place, and belongs in our celebrations as surely as we do.

34

35

36

The importance of the personal symbol (the chair) and function of the one who presides should not be underrated or underplayed.

The ambo should be beautifully designed, constructed of fine materials, and proportioned carefully and simply for its function.

New baptismal fonts should be constructed to allow for the immersion of infants.

Planning for a convergence of pathways to the liturgical space in a concourse or foyer or other place adequate for gathering before or after liturgies is recommended. Such a gathering space can encourage the building of the kind of community sense and feeling recognized now to be a prerequisite of good celebration.

38

39

The most powerful experience of the sacred is found in the celebration and the persons celebrating, that is, it is found in the action of the assembly: the living words, the living gestures, the living sacrifice, the living meal.

NOTES TO ILLUSTRATIONS

The numbers refer to the photograph numbers

1. Hancock Shaker village, Massachusetts.

2. Cloister, Saint John's Abbey and University Church, Collegeville, Minnesota. *architect:* Marcel Breuer. *Abbot:* Right Reverend Baldwin Dworshak, O.S.B.

3, 4. Saint Richard's Church, Jackson, Mississippi. *architect:* Thomas Biggs F.A.I.A. of Biggs, Weir, Neal and Chastain. *consultant:* Frank Kacmarcik. *Pastor:* Right Reverend Monsignor Josiah Chatham

5. Church of Saint Rita, Cottage Grove, Minnesota. *architect:* Theodore Butler of Hammel, Green and Abrahamson. *Pastor:* Reverend John Brandes

6. Saint Mary's Church, Edgefield, South Carolina. *design:* Frank Kacmarcik. *Pastor:* Reverend E. Christopher Lathem

7, 8. New Melleray Abbey Church, Dubuque, Iowa. *See below.*

9, 10. Saint Paul's Church, Minnesota City, Minnesota. *design:* Frank Kacmarcik. *Pastor:* Reverend George Moudry

11. Church of the Risen Savior, Apple Valley, Minnesota. *architect:* John Rauma F.A.I.A. of Griswold and Rauma Architects Inc. *consultant:* Frànk Kacmarcik. *Pastor:* Reverend Frederick T. Cussler

12, 13, 14, 15, 16, 17, 18, 19. Saint Mark's Church, Shakopee, Minnesota. built in 1862–68. *renovation design:* Frank Kacmarcik. *Pastor:* Reverend Francis J. Eret

20, 21, 22, 23, 24. New Melleray Abbey Church, Dubuque, Iowa, designed in 1867 by John Mullany, a student of

Augustus Welby Pugin. *initial restoration studies:* Willoughby
Marshall. *design and development:* Frank Kacmarcik and
Theodore Butler of Hammel, Green and Abrahamson.
Abbot: Right Reverend David Wechter, O.C.S.O. ,

25, 26, 27, 28, 29. Church of Saint John the Evangelist,
Hopkins, Minnesota. *architect:* George Rafferty of Rafferty,
Rafferty and Mikutoski and Associates. *consultant:* Frank
Kacmarcik. *Pastor:* Reverend W. Leo Howley

30. Church of the Risen Savior, *op. cit.*

31. Saint Richard's Church, *op. cit.*

32. Saint John the Baptist Church, Webster, Wisconsin.
sculptor: Gerald Bonnette. *Pastor:* Reverend Joseph Kelchak

33. Saint Thomas More Church, Brookings, South Dakota.
design: Frank Kacmarcik. *Pastor:* Reverend Monsignor John
McEneany

34. Saint Jude's Church, Grand Rapids, Michigan. *sculptor:*
Gerald Bonnette. *Pastor:* Reverend Monsignor Charles
Brophy

35. Church of the Risen Savior, *op. cit.*

36. Saint Mary's Church, Grand Forks, North Dakota.
design: Frank Kacmarcik. *Pastor:* Reverend Monsignor David
J. Boyle

37. Saint John the Baptist Church, New Brighton,
Minnesota. *architects:* Shifflet and Hutchinson. *design:*
Frank Kacmarcik. *Pastor:* Reverend Monsignor Paul J.
Koscielniak

38. Church of the Risen Savior, *op. cit.*

39. Church of the Resurrection, Portsmouth, Virginia.
architect: Dan Griffin. *consultant:* Frank Kacmarcik. *Pastor:*
Reverend Thomas J. Caroluzza

INDEX